A SPIRITUAL GUIDE TO MENTAL CLARITY

7 DAYS
TO MENTAL & SPIRITUAL FAST

RESET - RENEW - BALANCE - SELF-CARE

DE'ANGELA PIPPEN

7 Days To Mental & Spiritual Fast

Copyright © 2019 by De'Angela Pippen. All rights reserved. This book or any portion thereof may not be reproduced or used in any manner whatsoever without the express written permission of the publisher except for the use of brief quotations in a book review.

Book Cover Picture by De'Angela Pippen. All Graphics and Promotional by Enterpromedia, LLC.

Edited by Brinkley Fuller

Printed in the United States of America

First Printing, 2019

ISBN 978-0-578-57083-9

Enterpromedia, LLC

Birmingham, Alabama

For Books, Promotional Materials and Bookings, contact De'Angela Pippen.

www.deangelapippen.com

info@deangelapippen.com

PREFACE

A spiritual guide to mental clarity for the mind and spirit. This book provides tools and resources to help you prepare your journey through fasting and building a better YOU.

As a busy professional, your mind needs a break from running constantly! We all need to stay motivated and uplifted. It is necessary to take mental breaks.

I pray this book helps you in many ways. I have made it convenient to write down your feelings and thoughts after each chapter to guide you through your journey.

Thanks to God and my loved ones who have kept me together during the difficult times in my life. God bless those who have touched my life and have supported me throughout my journey in life. As I present my first book, I believe this guide will lead you to your mental and spiritual clarity.

DAY 1

REALIZATION

Have you felt uneasy because life seems to overwhelm you? Maybe anxiety? Depression? For me, I become angry and easily irritated. The feeling of uneasiness takes over and suddenly I feel mentally exhausted! We can't let emotions get the best of US.

It's now time to be intentional in creating mental and spiritual clarity in your life. The very first thing to do is: **1.** Take breaks from distractions. **2.** Take time to fast from things you are addicted to. (Fasting is not always related to religious purposes.)

Social Media is the first thing I recommend to fast from. Social Media has dictated every aspect of our life. It has affected our friendship, work, personal, and business life. As a business owner, I have learned to take breaks. I have found ways of promoting my business without spending all day on social media and set boundaries for my clients.

It is very important to take a few days to unwind and let go of things that affect your mental clarity. Your mind will greatly appreciate you in the long term. YOU matter most, more than anything. Staying focus is the key to a better YOU. Without focus, there's no you, clients, family, business, and ultimately no <u>HAPPINESS!</u>

> First step to your mental and spiritual clarity is writing down everything that is hindering you or blocking you at this point. Be honest with YOURSELF. (Your own personal journal section is on the next page.)

"The world will continue to go on, but your world will wait after you realize it's time to recharge your life." - Dee Pippen

REALIZATION JOURNAL

_____

_____

_____

_____

_____

_____

_____

_____

_____

_____

_____

_____

_____

DAY 2
SELF CHECK

Start this day with fresh air! Today, focus on checking YOU. Indeed, the problem can simply be you. We can be our own enemy and we're surprised when God reveal things concerning us. Yet, it does not devalue us as humans.

It is never too late to start the process of finding yourself again. By pacing yourself and practicing self-care, this will increase self-awareness about YOU. Taking aromatherapy bath allows you to spend time alone while embracing yourself. It's vital to take time for your spiritual and well-being.

Be creative by doing something different such as going to the spa or walking. Spend time reading the Bible and Self Help books to expand a better YOU. Writing is a great tool of expression that allows you to be free in your own right.

> Self-evaluation is a great way of educating who you are. Oftentimes, we blame others for things going wrong in our lives and don't take responsibility of our actions. In your spare time, write down your likes and dislikes about yourself. Remove people opinions and negativity from your mind. You will feel the release of those burdens with a clear mind and vision. Distractions will begin to fade out!

"Love who you are. If you don't like who you are figure out why not and work on loving you!" - Dee Pippen

SELF CHECK JOURNAL

DAY 3
KEEP GOING

How are the first few days going? Are you staying on track? Is your mindset coming alive?

Congratulations to you for starting your journey of spiritual mental clarity! This is the beginning of an awakening shift in your life. The tools provided in this book will be beneficial to you.

There are days when life gets hard and you will be tempted to go back to your old self. Sometimes, you will wonder if you are missing out. Just know things have not changed, but time. Do not allow the enemy to cause you to loose focus and distract you from your progress. You will be tested during your mental and spiritual cleansing process. When you realize your purpose, life becomes easier to navigate.

> List your accomplishments in your journal. It does not matter how big or small it is, it is a major accomplishment!

"When you feel like things are getting hard. Go harder for your purpose."- Dee Pippen

KEEP GOING JOURNAL

DAY 4
FULL DAY OF PRAYER

Are you ready? Now is the time for the real work. Let's start by writing down all of the toxic things such as people, situations, hurt and pain. It is time to establish a safe haven for your mind and spirit.

Gather your tools such as a fireproof ashtray to remove negativity. This represents letting go and not turning back. Release, relax, and relate by meditation. Meditate through prayer and cleansing of the spirit and mind.

Be intentional by setting up days for you to fully recharge. Create an atmosphere by playing soft music, taking a shower, and surrounding yourself with scented candles as the aroma shift the inner you. Set boundaries by taking breaks from the outside world.

Now, with your new mindset, you are able to identify the old thoughts patterns and leave it. Continue to renew your mindset with the Bible and scripture references. Creating affirmation builds mental toughness while confirming the new you.

> Be thankful to the most high for mental and spiritual clarity. Praise him for the transformation in your life. Let's begin new healthy eating habits and more importantly, filling your mind, body, and spirit with a new positive outlook.

"To get new results, one must try throwing away old ways of thinking and doing." - Dee Pippen

FULL DAY OF PRAYER JOURNAL

DAY 5
REFRESH...RENEW

Self-check is very important! Look into the mirror and admire YOU. You are a beautiful human being. You are unique and flawless. As you refresh and continue to renew, stay stress free from all toxicity.

It's important to surround yourself with the right people in your circle. Be there for the people who truly rock with you. It is vital to stay connected to your close family and friends who LOVES you for you! Remember, energy doesn't lie. If you feel unsettled around people, then it's best to remove yourself. Stay grounded with self-control.

Challenge yourself to experience nature's best. Go outside and let your feet sink into the ground whether it's grass, dirt, or sand. Breathe and allow the universe to fill you. Close your eyes and practice the square breathing technique. Square breathing technique consists of 4 counts of breathing. Inhale 4 counts and exhale 4 counts. Repeat up to 4 times.

> Write in your journal on any thoughts you're having. What makes you feel refreshed? Renewed? What keeps your spirit uplifted?

"To renew your mind, YOU must renew your spirit." - *Dee Pippen*

REFRESH…RENEW JOURNAL

DAY 6
POSITIVE AFFIRMATIONS

Hey you, you're almost there! You're one day away from completion. Do you feel more peaceful? Is your skin glowing? Are you happier?

Let's celebrate! You did not give up and you did not give in. Let's take an hour-long walk while reflecting the progress you've made. Increase healthy food intake and drink plenty of water. The body is the temple and it is very important to take care of it from mental clarity to daily exercise.

Continuous affirmation will get you through your daily life. It is vital to write down 20 affirmations ranging from success, health, personal, and business. Here's some examples to start with: "I am beautiful.", "I shall be enough!", "I will be a goddess.", "I am successful!", and "I shall accomplish everything I set out to do!". Set new goals for yourself with a clear conscious mindset.

> As the day comes to an end, take a bath with scented candles and soft music. After you air dry, look into the mirror and tell yourself: "I am taking

care of my mental and physical health.", "I believe in myself.", "I shall speak life into myself.", "I will prepare myself for my new journey." and "I love who I am and all that I am.".

"I AM - I SHALL - I WILL!" - Dee Pippen

POSITIVE AFFIRMATIONS JOURNAL

DAY 7
PEACE AND COMPLETION

Today is the day! This is the day of completion. You did it! It's time to rise and shine and take over the world!

How are you feeling? Exhale! Write down your experience and evaluate the things you have learned about YOU. Reflect on new peace, happiness, and harmony.

> Take a lavender shower to release stress and focus on the art of letting go. Connect with close friends. Enjoy nature's fresh air with a hit of sun. Start your newfound freedom, for you are complete!

"You are your own creator of your mental peace. You are the leader of your role to mental completion." - Dee Pippen

PEACE AND COMPLETION JOURNAL

_____
_____
_____
_____
_____
_____
_____
_____
_____
_____
_____
_____
_____
_____

FROM THE AUTHOR

I love you and I am so proud of you! Remember to speak life and not death. Your words are powerful. Keep your soul open. Follow your intuition. Follow your heart. Stay positive. I hope this helps you and may God bless you!

AROMATHERAPY BATH RECIPE

First, pray over you and bless the water.

Use warm water
Prepare bath with herbal ingredients of your choice
A tablespoon of real red or pink rose buds or petals
Sea Salt

Lavender

Add all ingredients to the warm water

Boil herbs for 5-9 minutes and add to the warm bath water.

Soak in bath water for 20 minutes.

Add meditation, light candles with soft music and relax.

Air-dry once you're finished.

www.ingramcontent.com/pod-product-compliance
Lightning Source LLC
Chambersburg PA
CBHW050708160426
43194CB00010B/2047